DEDICATION

I DEDICATE THIS BOOK
TO MY DAUGHTER,
KYLEIGH, WHO STANDS
AS MY INSPIRATION FOR
JUSTICE AND ACCOUNTABILITY.

Book Cover by Kevin Conwell, Sr.

Illustrations by Kevin Conwell, Sr.

979-8-9873400-0-4 edition 2023

Hi friends!
My name is Kyleigh.
Can I tell you about
my daddy?
My daddy,
I love my
daddy.

We are more than your favorite superheroes favorite superhero.

We are fierce, phenomenal, and fearfully and wonderfully made.

My daddy and me are one of a kind.

Some kids want to be firefighters, doctors, or teachers.

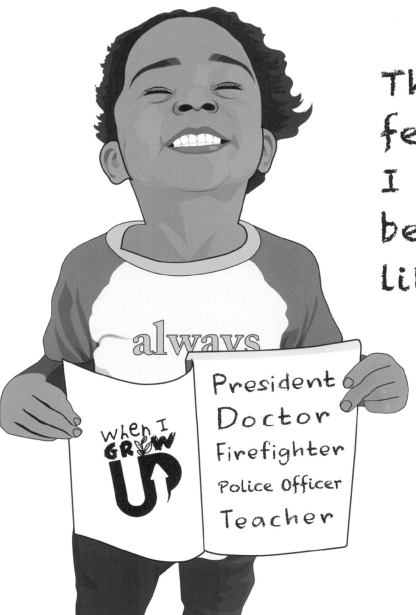

There are a few things that I want to be besides being like my Daddy.

My daddy tells me that he had dreams of me from the moment he met my mommy.

He says he
dreams
about my
dreams and
hopes.

I respond,

"I'm just Kyleigh."

But he says,

"You are so much more."

Why can't my daddy understand I'm only four?

But he says, "I always wanted more from the time Cupid struck me on the dance floor."

As corny as my dad was, my mommy gave him a chance, and from that moment on, they found their rhythm in life and began to dance.

Four years later, I was born.

I was the missing piece that made this happy house a home.

We do everything together.

Daddy won three awards for his public relations work for attorneys fighting for social justice. He said, "You and your mommy are my reason why."

Daddy says, "I dream about the world my Kyleigh will change."

Acknowledgments

Thank you to everyone who has poured into my life. I am an inspiration to many because you all wrapped your loving arms around me.

Mom, thank you for planting the seed of vision and teaching me to work towards my aspirations regardless of the obstacles.

Karen, your vision for us transformed me and the world around us. And where would I be without the guy in the sky?

Thank you, God, for your unwavering love and protection.

This book exists because of You!

Kevin Conwell Sr. is a marketing strategist with a passion for the community. He is the chairman of The Conwell Group, LLC., a modern-day consulting and communications holding company. Additionally, Kevin is the founder of both Wake Hustle Grind for Profit and Wake Hustle Grind Non-Profit. He is the CEO and lead graphic designer/creative director for 3kpmarketing.com.

Since 2007, Kevin has successfully managed a full-service advertising agency catering to Government Agencies, Non-Profit Organizations, Tech Startups, Fortune 100 companies, and Small Business Startups.

He has overseen projects totaling over $500 million throughout the United States and internationally. Kevin earned his BA in Marketing from Cleveland State University.

He actively engages in mentorship, coaching, educational teaching, training, workshops, and providing human services to youth and adults to enhance their quality of life.

Email: info@kevinconwell.com
Social Media: @Wakehustlegrind_ceo
Website: www.KevinConwell.com

www.wakehustlegrind.com

Dontaye Carter is a communication strategist and content creator passionate about storytelling. Dontaye graduated from Florida A&M University, where he studied Broadcast Journalism.

Before graduating, Dontaye worked as a video editor, Producer, and Executive Producer. He later transitioned to working on-air as a reporter.

After hanging up his microphone, Dontaye led the Publication Relations Department for the Fulton County District Attorney's office before starting his firm, Carter Media Group. Dontaye worked with the attorneys representing the victims' families in the Surviving R Kelly case. He was also one of the communication strategists hired to help raise awareness about the Ahmaud Arbery case. He began writing "My Daddy and Me" in 2022 with his daughter Kyleigh. For many of the national cases that Dontaye has worked on, Kyleigh has been by his side. This book was birthed out of Dontaye and Kyleigh's discussions about building a better world. Dontaye is passionate about mentoring, community building, and changing the narrative around Black men and fatherhood.

Email: Dontaye@Cartermedia.net
Social Media: @MyDaddyAndMeBook
Website: www.MyDaddyAndMeBook.com

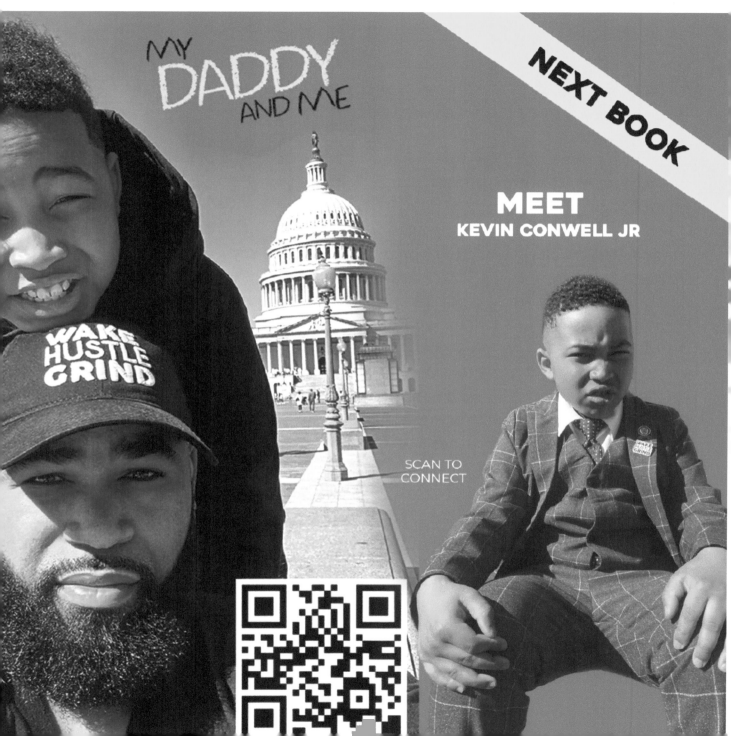